This Book

Belongs To

MW00949462

Made in the USA
Monee, IL
03 July 2022

99014887R00073